Journal Bliss

Creative Prompts to Unleash Your Inner Eccentric

Violette

NORTH LIGHT BOOKS
Cincinnati, Ohio

www.mycraftivity.com

13 12 11 10 09   5 4 3 2 1

Distributed in Canada by Fraser Direct
100 Armstrong Avenue
Georgetown, ON, Canada L7G 5S4
Tel: (905) 877-4411

Distributed in the U.K. and Europe by David & Charles
Brunel House, Newton Abbot, Devon, TQ12 4PU, England
Tel: (+44) 1626 323200, Fax: (+44) 1626 323319
E-mail: postmaster@davidandcharles.co.uk

Distributed in Australia by Capricorn Link
P.O. Box 704, S. Windsor, NSW 2756 Australia
Tel: (02) 4577-3555

Library of Congress Cataloging-in-Publication Data

Violette.
  Journal bliss : creative prompts to unleash your inner
eccentric / Violette.
     p. cm.
  ISBN 978-1-60061-189-6 (pbk. : alk. paper)
  1. Handicraft. 2. Diaries. 3. Artists' books. I. Title.
  TT149.V56 2009
  745.5--dc22
                          2008042499

Editor
Jessica Strawser

Designer
Geoff Raker

Photographer
Adam Hand

Production Coordinator
Greg Nock

fw media
www.fwmedia.com

Contents

Introduction

> *"When you follow your bliss ... doors will open where you would not have thought there would be doors; and where there wouldn't be a door for anyone else."*
>
> — Joseph Campbell

I invite you to join me—don a pair of magical boots and come along on an exhilarating adventure to find Journal Bliss. It doesn't matter if your magical boots are real or imaginary; all we have to do is let go and listen to our intuition, and they will guide our steps on an amazing creative journey. These magical boots are resplendent in color, sprinkled with glitter, words of encouragement and love. Donning them gives us permission to be ourselves and to express ourselves fully and fearlessly through our own creativity.

The transformative abilities of art making are undeniable. If you have any doubt, just watch children working on finger paintings and proudly showing off their exuberant creations. The light and joy in their eyes demonstrate the unrestrained self-expression that brought them to a place of pure bliss. In my own personal journey, I have found that art has taken me places where nothing else could. But it was not until seven years ago that I discovered the magical elixir: combining visual art with words.

Apart from my art making, I had been journaling traditionally, with words, but would often find myself stuck in one place, like a scratch on a record. I felt powerless to move forward. During one such stuck moment on a particularly sad day, I grabbed a clean journal page, drew my face, painted it blue and added some words to describe how I was feeling. I began drawing and creating a collage of more pictures, and before I knew it I was moving rapidly through the place of "stuckness" to one of bliss and joy. Eureka!

I was so excited by my discovery that I wanted to share it with as many people as I could. Since that time I have taught hundreds of women and children to create a visual journal for self-expression and understanding. When you journal in a visual way, you bypass the conscious mind and travel straight to your subconscious, mining it for its treasures.

In these pages I will teach you how to do all this and more: to create juicy backgrounds, doodle to your heart's content (even if you thought you never could), and craft your own lettering to fashion personal, artistic pages full of meaning. You'll learn that almost anything can become an idea for a journal page. You'll learn to silence your inner critic and create freely. And you'll get plenty of inspiration for conjuring up dazzling journal pages when your creative well runs dry.

So tie on your magical boots and get ready to follow your bliss on this amazing journey into your own heart and soul. You'll leave a trail of glitter in your wake for others to follow!

Yummy Supplies

fluid acrylics

acrylic Paints

twinkling H₂O's

Shimmering pots of juiciness!

glitter

WATER SOLUBLE OIL PASTELS

Portfolio Oil Pastel

micron Pens

Brush

Charcoal pencil

Pencil

MICRON

MICRON 05

Watercolour pencil crayon

White eraser

HB

glitter glue

ckles

PoRTable CReaTiviTy

Be Ready all the time foR wheN the muse Comes to Visit with a PoRtable Creativity kit!

Small container foR water

eraser

water color pencil Crayons

pencil

Brush

I'm PoRTable!

tiny water Color set

Sketch Pad

You CaN Sketch in coffee Shops, Restaurants, doctoR's office, airpoRt, dentist's waiting roomo oR wherever you find yourself with Some free time.

If you are sketching iN NatuRe put youR artful gear in a knapsack!

feed me!

Remember to bring a Snack and Something to drink!

Peace

H₂O

Have fuN!

Silencing Your Inner Critic

> *"And now here is my secret, a very simple secret:*
> *It is only with the heart that one can see clearly;*
> *what is essential is invisible to the eye."*

∞ Antoine de Saint-Exupéry, *The Little Prince*

Do you have that little critical inner voice that tells you you're not good enough or not talented enough, or that warns you not to take risks? I always think of my inner critic in the fitting term coined by noted counselor and personal and executive coach Richard Carson: the gremlin (in fact, he wrote a book called *Taming Your Gremlin* and is founder of the Gremlin Taming Institute). Regardless of what you call this voice, everyone has one.

Art journaling is a good way to silence your inner critic. Rather than ignoring him when you begin your art journal (which can be easier said than done!), try starting by giving him a voice on a journal page. It can be a visual voice, a literal voice or both. If you can have a dialogue with this critic and actually imagine him outside of yourself, then you can separate that voice from your own. You become able to see that what the critic says to you is no longer relevant.

What does your inner voice look like? Is it male or female? What color is it? If it had a name what would it be? Draw your inner critic and include a dialogue with him on the page. Then, when he has had his say, turn to a clean page and get ready to begin!

HOW do YOU EAT AN elephant?

— ouch!

ONE Bite at a time! Take art making 1 step at a time. Begin with practicing doodling, making faces, drawing from nature, make BoRDees, create Backgrounds Practice drawing *flourishes* then put it all together! there... now wasn't that *easier* than you thought?

I'm over-whelmed
just take one step at a time
But I'm not talented
oh yes you are... you just have to find your
groove
YOU CAN DO it!
how do I find my Style?
By trying different Styles & combining them...
yours will emerge!
How can I get better?
By lots of practice and not being afraid of making mistakes

What to Journal...

about...

- around a quotation that speaks to your heart ♥
- a list of things you love
- to illustrate a story like the "Strapless ballgown"
- to celebrate someone special
- to document a feeling you want to give life to
- to pour out onto the page a jumble of feelings
- to teach yourself to be in the moment with nature
- as a way to remember your travels
- a letter to yourself
- a stream of consciousness Rambling... blah, blah, blah...
- to work out a problem or concern
- to try out different materials and techniques

Plus: it's cheap therapy!

CORE Beliefs

Believe that Life is worth Living, AND YOUR Belief Will help create the fact —WILLIAM JAMES

if I have the belief that I can do it, I Shall Surely acquire the capacity to do it EVEN if I may not have it At the Beginning. —mahatma GANDHi ♥

I Believe thAt EVERY PERSON is BORN With talent —maya Angelou

15

A B C D E F G H I J K L M N O P Q R S T U V W X Y Z

Creating Your Own Fanciful Lettering

Fanciful Lettering

A musician must make music, an artist must paint, a poet must write if he is to be ultimately at peace with himself.

— Abraham Maslow

From the exquisite markings of the ancient Sanskrit writings to modern-day text, humans have always been fascinated by the art of making marks to communicate their thoughts and ideas. Incorporating lettering as part of our artwork is a natural extension of this, and an important part of visual journaling.

When I was a teenager I bought a Speedball lettering book, some ink pens and nibs and began trying to imitate proper, perfect letter forms. Try as I might, I was unsuccessful. Number one, I don't like following rules, and number two, I'm not much of a perfectionist (in fact, I've abolished that word from my vocabulary!). I sure wish I had had a teacher back then who had encouraged me to develop my own style of lettering and toss out the rules. Instead, it took me a couple of decades before I gave myself permission to develop my very own fanciful lettering.

Years ago I began drawing and selling cartoons. I amassed a number of cartooning books with instructions on how to letter in a cartoon style, and from them I learned how to fit the letters into one another to make the words appear more personal and finished. But most of all, I learned that creating your own lettering is so much more fun than struggling with formal letter forms!

Developing your own style of lettering is a fun way of personalizing your journal pages and adding a wonderful artsy dimension to your work. That's not to say you can't use computer-generated journaling, or even words and phrases clipped from books and magazines—but if that's your style, try using artistic hand-lettering in combination with these methods to add your own *je ne sais quoi* to your work!

The best way to get to the place where you like your printing and writing is simply to practice. My mom, who is an avid scrapbooker, used to constantly say that she could not use her handwriting in her pages—it was illegible. I encouraged her to practice, and she began using a light box to trace my words (she really likes my swirly lettering). Before you know it she could handwrite her pages as well as doodle along the borders freehand! If my mom can do it, so can you!

Let's take a look at some ways to create your own lettering and experiment with a variety of tools in order to add your own inimitable imprint to your artwork.

Try nibs of different sizes
Kerning - in cartoonist speak
it means fitting letters into
each other - adjusting the spaces.
this adds interest and
variety to your journal
pages !

Lettering can be

illuminated... there are no
rules in this playground - fun !

Be free ENJOY
JUMP SKIP → WOODEN Skewer
SING DANCE

UNabashed

experiment ← Brush
be the Creative Being
that you ARE!

Bliss Joy ABundance

Gratitude Play Explore!

Let Silly in! Love Laugh

Live Be Joyful ♥ SPRead your Wings

Mix ScRipt and PRinting TogetHeR

Just foR fun! HaVe fuN

Spill OpeN Allow Let it Be

Don't woRRy ABout Being Messy

Life iS Messy & very Real "and juicy"

EmBrace it All...the good and

the so-called Bad ★ hold a space for

WOndeR to move into...it's Magic

imagine JOY Peace

Love abundace

PASSiON Bliss

aRT SPiRit fly

heart create

Dance Sing SKiP

Gratitude

make SWIRLY headlines
OR
BLOCK headings

create wavy lines AND WRite insiDe
the LiNES. thERE ARE No RuLES really
with the exception of having FuN! GO foR it!

WRap text around your image oR Photo foR interest...write oR PRiNt

I want the Whole enchilada...

in life I want the whole ENchilada—that means i want it all! I want to experience the highs and the lows, I want to experience Life in all its fullness

KEEP YOUR fACE to the SunShine and YOu will NeVeR See thE ShaDoW

-helen keller

26

PEACE of Mind

Peace of mind seems to be what I'm always after. When someone asks me what I want for a gift I almost always say PEACE of mind. I just came back from a massage appointment and my therapist made me count my breath. She knows that I need to find that place of Peace. Part of what I need is to get to a place of acceptance

...the TOYS would SPRING to Life after the children AND ADULTS WOULD LEAVE the house

Bodacious Borders

" I found I could say things with color and shapes that I couldn't say any other way — things I had no words for. "

∞ Georgia O'Keeffe

I have a fascination with borders. Even though I don't like to be "boxed in" or "pigeon-holed" (or any of those other clichés) I still enjoy adding borders of some form to many of my journal pages. Perhaps I'm trying to contain my illustrations so they won't run off the page and escape. Do you remember the old *Merrie Melodies* cartoons in which toys would spring to life after the children and adults would leave the house? To this day I believe that the inanimate objects in my home come to life when I am not looking. How else can you explain a chair poised in a jaunty fashion, ready to make a run for it, frozen forever in time since I disturbed its escape? But I digress …

Borders have an appealing decorative quality to them that finishes off a page beautifully. They can help anchor a page so that your words or images aren't floating in the air. Not that floating is a bad thing; sometimes you might choose to have your images floating, and other times you might not. Whatever floats your boat!

If you suffer from the most common of afflictions that creatives suffer from—fear of the blank page—adding a border to a prepared background dispels some of that fear. Once you have a border, you're already on your way, and you've made the journey a bit more inviting, too!

BLACK and WHITE
fanciful borders

draw checkerboards

Scallops are fun to draw!

Practice drawing different columns

FUNKY SCRAPE PAINTED BORDERS

Scrape paint with credit card

Splatter OR flick Paint

Divide PAPER into borders

doodle and write in BORDERS

BLiSS ♥ JOY
Peace Love Joy

Cut in Strips

Peace Love Bliss

BLISS Love Joy Passion

33

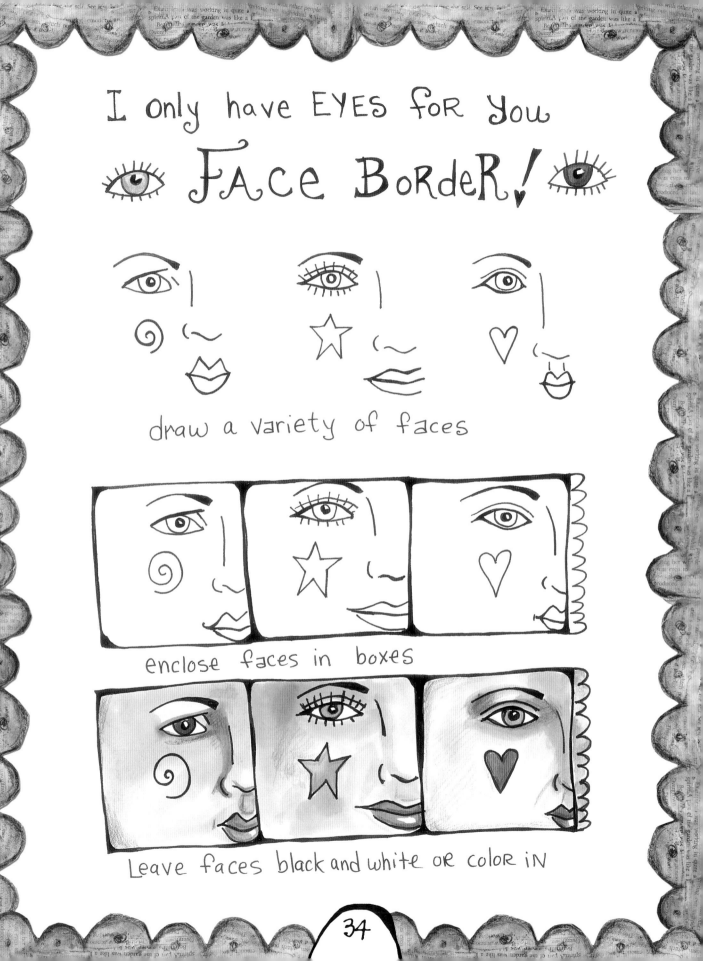

I only have EYES for You
FACE BORDER!

draw a variety of faces

enclose faces in boxes

Leave faces black and white or color in

35

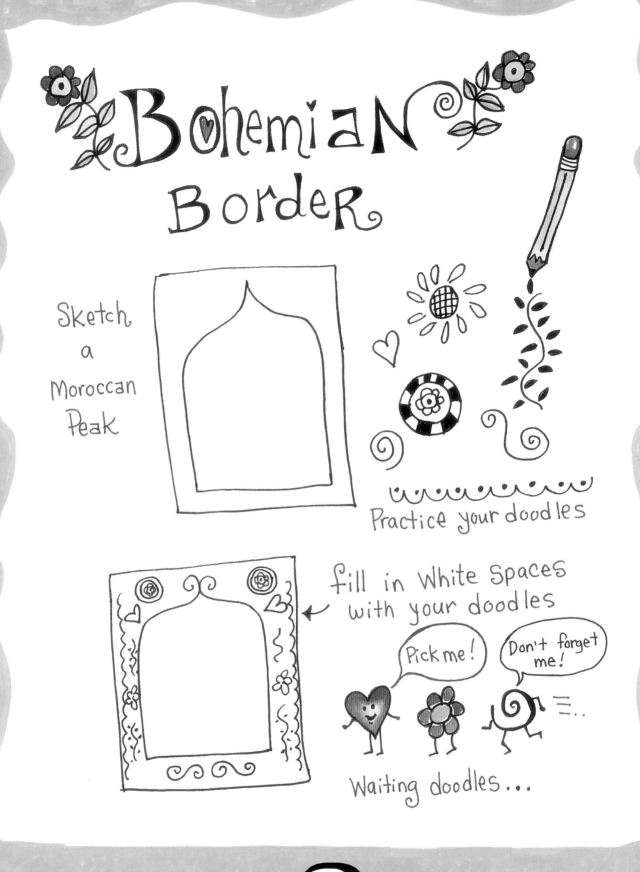

Bohemian Border

Sketch a Moroccan Peak

Practice your doodles

fill in White spaces with your doodles

Pick me!

Don't forget me!

Waiting doodles...

House Border

Paint Back-
ground

Stencil Pattern
with Sequin waste

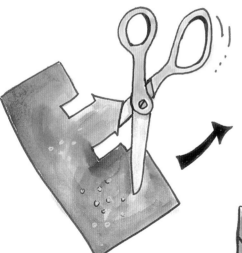

Cut house shapes

glue to
painted
background

- Stamp circles
with lid

PATCHWORK
BORDER

Cut and tear pieces of your Background papers

peac Love jo Passion Blis.

Love is

You can use Photocopies

DRaw a face on Scrap paper, cut out

glue to paper -add dimension to face and ragged border with charcoal Pencil

Doodling

" *When my daughter was about seven years old, she asked me one day what I did at work. I told her I worked at the college—that my job was to teach people how to draw. She stared back at me, incredulous, and said, 'You mean they forget?'* "

∽ Howard Ikemoto

Who doesn't love to doodle? How many times have you sat at your desk or kitchen table during a long phone call, pen in hand, and wound up with some pretty phantasmagorical doodles? Now don't tell me you can't draw or doodle—of course you can! Your doodles can be windows to your soul.

When I went back to college in my mid-thirties, I couldn't decide whether to major in psychology or art, so I took classes in both. The notepad for my academic subjects was peppered with so many faces, arrows and other doodles that there was barely room for writing. The arrows were shooting off in every direction. In Harry Nilsson's epic song "Land of the Point," he says, "A point in every direction is like no point at all." So my point is—ha!—that I didn't have any direction! Eventually I realized that art was my true love. You will note, however, that psychology has crept into my work as well. Visual journaling for me has been a vehicle to move toward my bliss, and a totally transformative and life-affirming experience.

When you doodle absentmindedly, you relinquish control of your left brain and allow your right brain to take over. That's when the magic happens. Doodling while you are sitting in a classroom or meeting, talking on the telephone or waiting in a waiting room is a good start. Now, if you must watch TV (and occasionally I do), grab a pad and a pen or pencil and, while watching your program, aimlessly begin doodling—anything. I've found that often my doodles relate to the subject matter of the program, whether they're patterns, objects or even faces. The trick is not to judge yourself at all while you draw. Just have fun and play! It's all about exploring your creativity.

The following pages are designed to inspire you to let go and doodle to your heart's content. When you're ready to move on from mindless doodling to *mindful* doodling, begin by practicing drawing anything that you find yourself drawn to. Eventually you will notice that your own symbology or imagery will emerge. In my artwork, you'll notice that I love using spirals, hearts (both flying and stationary), stars, moons, columns, faces and flowers. Begin sketching without judgment, and let your inner world have a voice!

Waiting at the airport

I love watching people get excited to see their relatives and friends arrive

girl waiting for relatives to arrive.
it feels like I've been practically living here. I'm drawing this standing up so it's a wee bit messy.

← I lost my subject. Sometimes you have to draw quickly.
- Lots of planes coming in from **Asia**
- it Doesn't matter what nationality you are - you are always :joyful: to see your loved ones after a long absence

Love is the same everywhere

okay... now I'm getting Really BOReD !!!

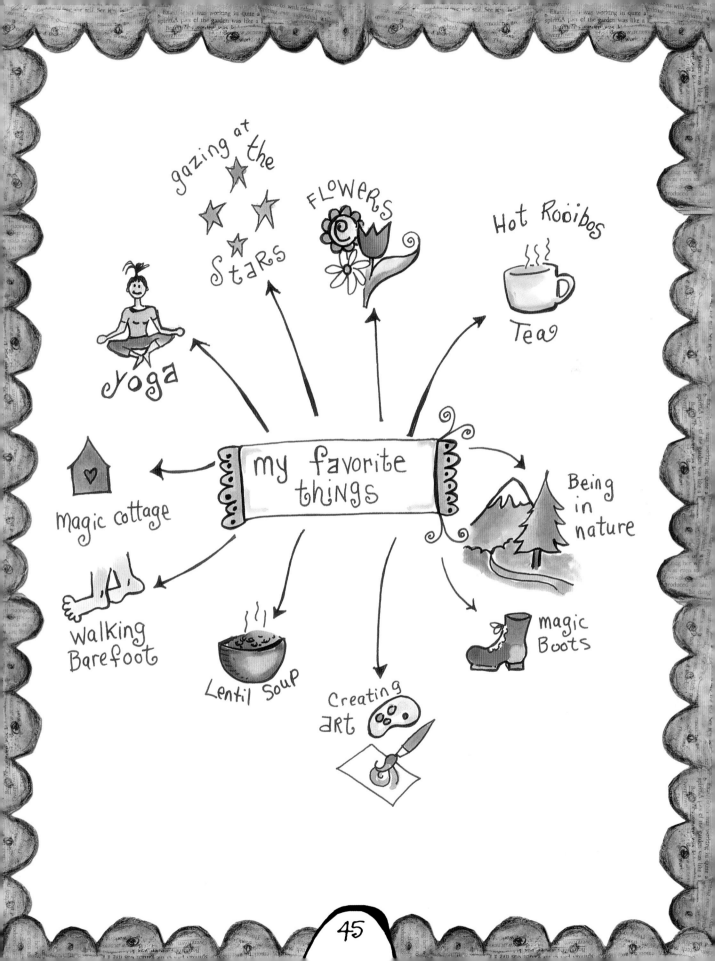

gazing at the Stars

FLOWERS

Hot Rooibos Tea

yoga

Magic cottage

my favorite things

Being in nature

Walking Barefoot

Lentil Soup

Creating art

magic Boots

Drawing in Nature

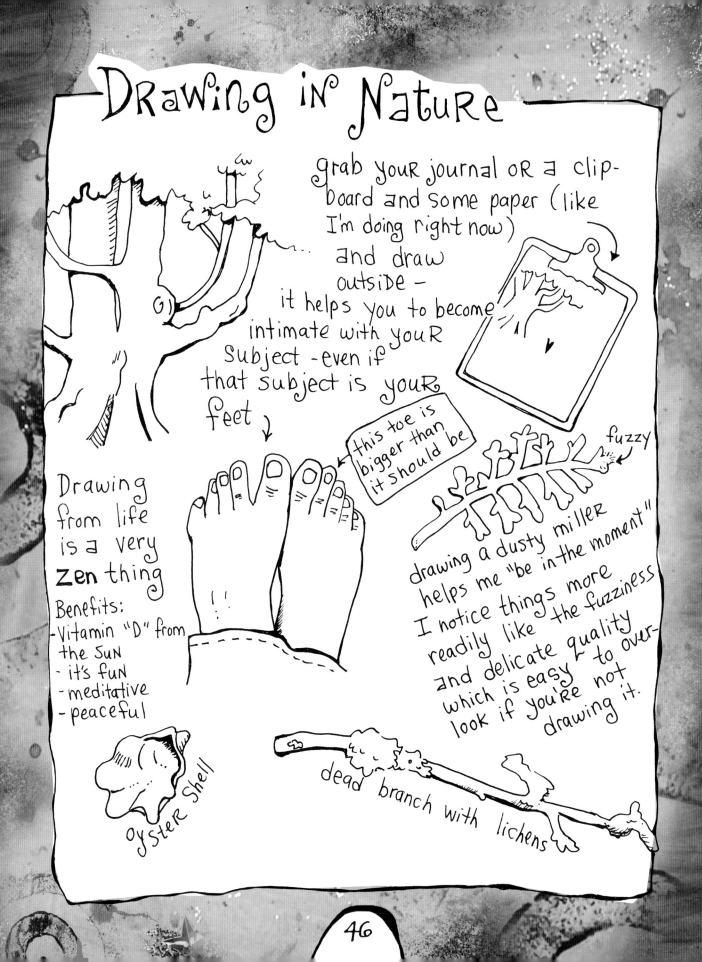

grab your journal or a clip-board and some paper (like I'm doing right now) and draw outside - it helps you to become intimate with your subject - even if that subject is your feet ↓

this toe is bigger than it should be

Drawing from life is a very **zen** thing

Benefits:
- Vitamin "D" from the sun
- it's fun
- meditative
- peaceful

fuzzy

drawing a dusty miller helps me "be in the moment" I notice things more readily like the fuzziness and delicate quality which is easy to over-look if you're not drawing it.

oyster shell

dead branch with lichens

drawing

Journaling

radio interviews

Creating youtube Videos

Facilitating Workshops

Blogging

magazines

Books

illustrating

Writing

eDucation

classes

Reading books

art magazines

online tutorials

aRtful Choices

Tools for Healing

The Welcoming Tree

This tree reminds me of the Friendly Giant where the Castle has all kinds of chairs and rockers to curl up in. The welcoming tree beckons you to sit, dream and be embraced by a loving presence.

WONDERFULLY spontaneous altars were found everywhere... like this one which contained rocks, a flower and a shell. One wonders what the intent of the creator was. It lent a magical quality to Hollyhock.

There were many stacked rocks everywhere.

Flourishes

When I was a little girl I used to play with my sister and playmates in an old, abandoned truck. Mint was growing around the truck in profusion. As we climbed in and out of the truck we rubbed against the mint, and the air was filled with its wonderful refreshing fragrance. To this day whenever I smell mint I'm transported back in time to when I was little, playing around the old truck. The mint plants were like flourishes: accenting and embracing the truck, rendering it more beautiful and inviting. The same goes for using flourishes in your art. You can enhance the focal point, whether it be a phrase or an image, by employing your very own fanciful doodles. Using flourishes in your visual journaling pages can add a cohesive element to otherwise disparate items. You can buy rub-on flourishes or even rubber stamps, but doodling your own flourishes makes your artwork that much more personal.

Start a file, box or scrapbook of flourishes and interesting doodles that you like clipped from magazines, junk mail or catalogs. Then, refer to your inspiration collection whenever you need ideas for your own doodles. First, try sketching them on a separate piece of paper. Do not judge yourself while you doodle—just have fun and draw quickly without giving it too much thought. When you've created some flourishes to your liking, you can re-create them on the pages of your art journal with a fine-tipped felt pen, ink pen or even white gel pens over colored backgrounds. Don't forget to make copies of your favorite flourishes and add them to your inspiration file so you can re-use or re-create them later in your artwork, collages or even image transfers (which we'll discuss later in this book).

FUN
with
FLOURISHES

mint was
growing around
the truck in profusion

Face Drawing tutorial

Start with an oval or circle

Segment it

Sketch in the facial features

add details erase lines

Practice drawing a variety of faces

making FACES colorful

PeN, watercolors, watercolor Pencil crayons, gel Pens

- PeN and pencil crayon

ink, PeN, watercolor, pencil crayon, oil pastels

PeN, felt PeN, Highlighters, Charcoal

PEN AND WATERCOLORS

LONG-necked gIRL

A couple of years ago I drew a long-necked face and put it up on my blog as a challenge to my readers. Many of them kept saying they couldn't draw faces, so I made it easy for them to download my image and then to either embellish it or to create their own versions. The results were amazing! I believe the simple challenge encouraged the readers of my blog to decorate their own long-necked girl and then go on to create their own unique faces. If you need a creative jump-start, why not try it for yourself?

a friend once asked me how did I find my style. It's not something you consc- iously seek out...it finds you

the trick is to not care what other people will say or think just listen to your heart. wear what makes your heart sing! ignore the fashion of the day— combine opposite colors and patterns just be your

find your style be brave have fun listen to your heart

I CARRY a few things close to my heart

even though it might Seem like i Share every single little Detail of my life i keep Some things to mySelf. WheRe is the mystery in telling all?

Groovy Backgrounds

> *Every artist dips his brush in his own soul,*
> *and paints his own nature into his pictures.*
>
> ∞ Henry Ward Beecher

I was born in Casablanca, the exotic, colorful city in Morocco (setting of the famous Humphrey Bogart film). With my Spanish roots and fascinating birthplace, it probably comes as no surprise that I am influenced by interesting and vibrant cultures and feel a kinship to the places that honor the creative, spiritual and passionate parts of ourselves. Where we are born—along with the other places we have traveled to that have captured our hearts—defines and shapes us. Our origins are like the backgrounds of our lives, the foundations that we build upon.

Similarly, artful backgrounds will enrich the pages of your art journal. As with borders, beginning by preparing a background can help those of us who have a fear of the blank page to move beyond that fear into a more intuitive place where we are guided by the stirrings of our souls. But unlike with borders, the result is already fully integrated into the piece you have yet to create.

In this chapter you will learn how to create your own backgrounds so that your visual journal pages will be imbued with your energy or essence. I'll illustrate simple and easily learned techniques such as scrape painting, Rorschach painting (no ink blot analysis required!), decorative painted backgrounds, patchwork paper collages and more!

Scrape Painting

Squirt Paint onto a piece of Paper

Using a credit card scrape paint around paper

You can add a second color when the first is dry or when wet. Scrape over your page

NAME
NOM

ToneD DoWN PainteD Backgrounds

LOUD
Paint background
with fluorescent
color

SuBdueD
- Paint over with
thinned gesso

⊚ ♡ Cut Shapes ☆ ☽ Layered tissue Collage

cut out desired Shape

glue to cardstock

glue scrunched tissue over top. randomly stroke thinned paint over tissue

63

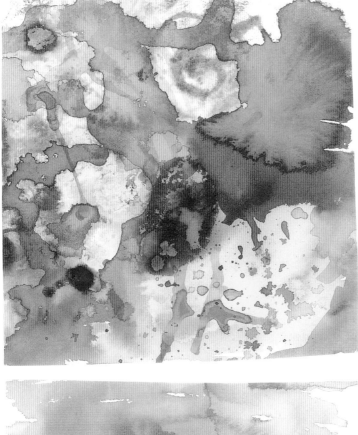

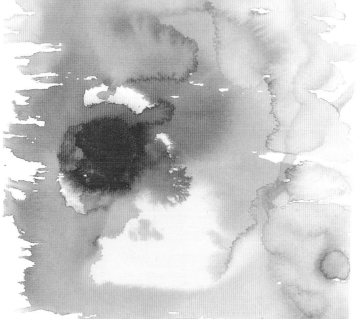

Splatter Painted Backgrounds

- Wet watercolor Paper with a brush

- Splatter thinned down acrylics, watercolors or fluid acrylics on wet PaPeR

- Color CoPY YouR BACKgrounds to use in future JouRnal pages OR use the original foR YouR creation!

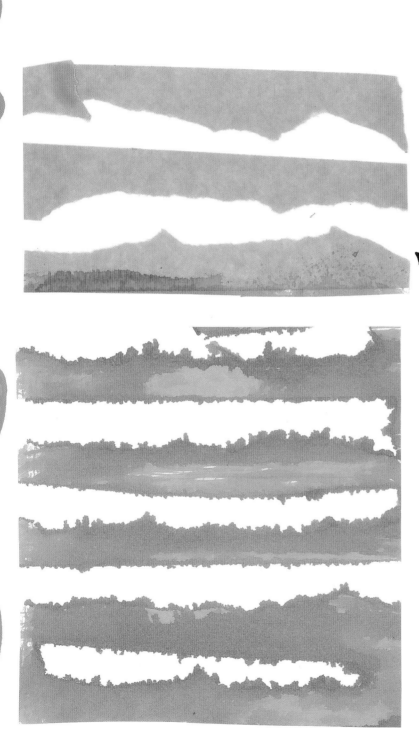

TORN masking Tape Background

← tear tape in strips and adhere to paper

- Brush on acrylic or water color paint

- Remove tape carefully.

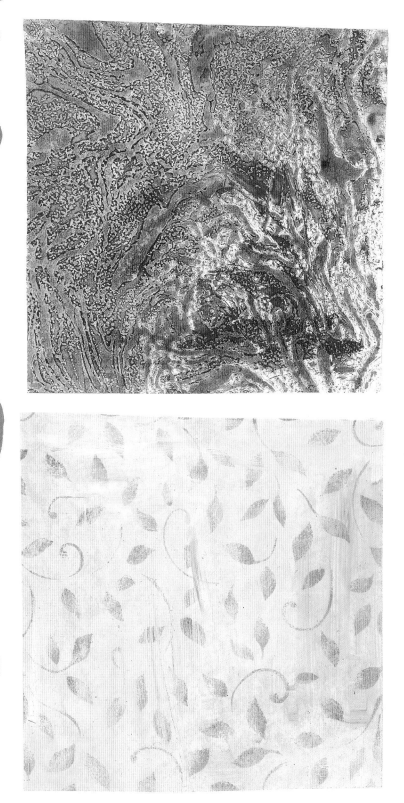

Wallpaper Backgrounds

acrylic
Paint brushed
over anaglypta
(textured wallpaper)

thinned acrylic
Paint brushed
over wallpaper

making textuReS

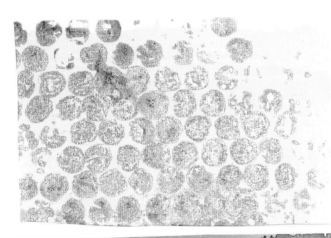

← BUBBLE WRAP
With metallic paint
over acrylic wash

↖ anaglypta
with metallic
paint over
acrylic wash

Gesso ON
INDIAN PaiSLEY
WOOD Stamp ↙

Rorschach Inkblot Background

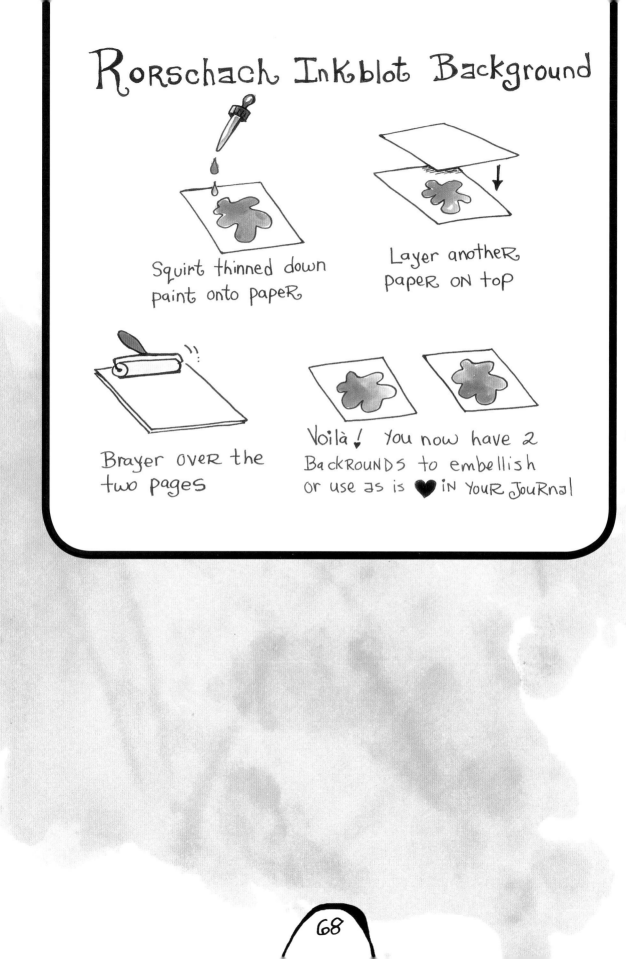

Squirt thinned down paint onto paper

Layer another paper on top

Brayer over the two pages

Voilà! You now have 2 backrounds to embellish or use as is ♥ in your journal

DyeD PAPeR towels

Scrunch up a  PapeR towel

Dip in pot of diluted paint

OPeN UP to reveal blank spots and  re-scrunch

Dip in Second CoLoR

UN-SCRUNCH to reveal cool mottled pattern

Decorative Backgrounds

Choose a simple
Pattern to repeat
Darken lines with
Black pen

Writing Backgrounds

when you follow your bliss all manner of miracles begin to happen. A book you need appears. The person you need info from calls you out of the blue, you receive unexpected money - all this happ

every morning I get up and walk outside and greet the day. then I put on the kettle to make tea. AfteR that I check my e-mails answer them then begin to draw. Sometimes I draw outside in the sun.

Write oR print your background in a stream of consciousness manner. Don't worry if it's not perfect. You'll be cutting, tearing and covering up much of youR Background. Just put your energy on it!

Take a step towards the universe and it takes a step towards you! It works! Really it does. How about this scenario: You turn on radio and the song comes on answering your question! I read once about a woman who couldn't decide if she should move to San Fransisco or New York. She gets in the car, turn on the radio — the first song to come on asks "If you're going to San Fransisco." That was the answer from the Universe / Spirit! The woman moved and has never looked back. There is an intelligence out the

Snazzy Stencils

negative

positive

negative

Rorschach Background

positive

leave white for journaling

RANDOM CRAZY QUILT
Background

use Pages toRN from Books too!

... fuRther embellished Crazy Quilt

dyed paper towel

MOD PODGE tissue and dyed PaPER towels over crazy Quilt Background

MOD PODGE

tissue

nurture

cel

delightful artful messengers

Funky Envelope Art

"Life is a luminous halo, a semi-transparent envelope surrounding us from the beginning."

☞ Virginia Woolf

Who doesn't love to receive a merry missive in the mail? What with the advent of e-mail and instant messaging, the art of letter writing is almost extinct. Whenever I receive a card or letter in the mail, I get so excited. Better yet to receive a decorated envelope—in fact, the envelope sometimes is more important or interesting than what lies within.

Twenty years ago, before the popularity of mail art, a young friend who I had met at college, Susanna, began mailing me letters that were packaged in the most whimsical envelopes—she had made each one a collage, drawing or glittery work of art. Every time I received one of these delightful artful messengers I jumped up and down with joy! Susanna was an art student, and creating art on envelopes was simply an extension of her creativity. Between assignments she would play with paper, pen and collage ephemera to invent unique envelope designs of her own. She started my fascination with the decorated envelope, and it has only grown in the decades since.

Try funkifying your store-bought envelopes by doodling a face or some of your favorite symbols anywhere you like—on the back, on the flap, on the front or even all over—with a black pen. Or, customize the design for the recipient. For example, if you and a friend are dieting together, you might decorate the envelope with drawings of fruits and vegetables along with some penned in motivational sayings, like "You can do it!" or "You go, girl!" If you want to take your creativity even further, create a template—or use the one I provide on page 84—and make your own envelope from scratch, shaped any way you like. It's the perfect functional use for your favorite borders, backgrounds and doodles.

Funky Envelopes

Doodle an image and words

Paint with medium of choice

Love Yourself

Creative Spirit...

DRAW, INK AND COLOR DOODLES, CUTOUT

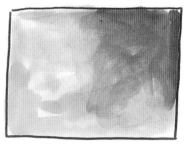

Paint envelope

Creative Spirit...

Assemble your cutout
doodles onto painted
background and glue.
You can add additional
doodles to envelope

gRaffiti envelope

fLy

Use crazy quilt background.
add a cutout zig zag border

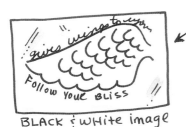

BLACK & WHITE image

Using packing tape image transfer technique
-glue over background

add doodles, words with pen and ink, Splatter ink
-tear a piece of paper for address, glue

give WiNGS to your SouL MAKE ART

follow your bliss fly

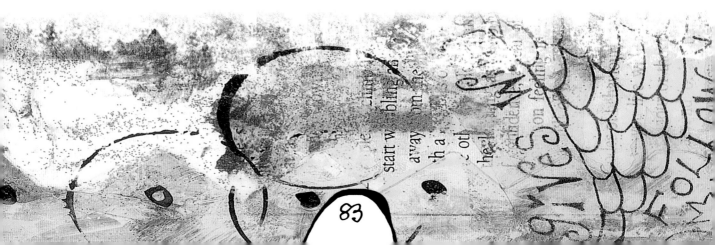

Make Your Own
Envelope
Template

a Creative Conversation

Sometimes I feel like I'm having a creative conversation with my 2 sides. the angelic side tells me to create art and be happy whereas my nasty side tells me to forget about it and wallow in self pity. I like my angelic side better!

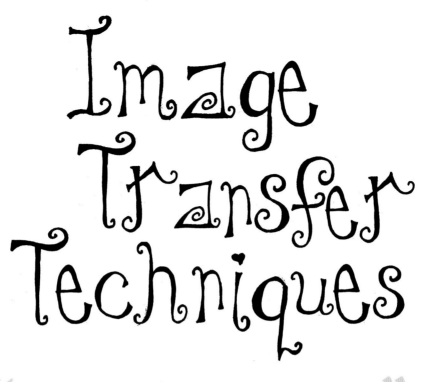

Image Transfer Techniques

"*You are always on your way to a miracle!*"

∞ Sark

Imagine being able to replicate some of the cool techniques you've seen in your favorite paper arts magazines. I've often been mystified when I've seen elaborate swirls and imagery superimposed over drawings, painted backgrounds or writing and wondered, "How did they *do* that?" Image transfers are a great way to add depth and texture to your journal pages. In this chapter you'll learn to transfer any image you like—be it a photo or an original work of art—onto the pages of your art journal in a way that allows the background of the page to show through. Whether you want your image to take the spotlight, to blend seamlessly with the rest of your page or to appear in a ghostly form over a painted background (as with the sketches I transferred to the piece on the opposite page), you can achieve it with a simple image transfer method.

The possibilities are truly as far reaching as your imagination. (For examples of journal pages featuring image transparencies, see pages 76 and 101; packing tape transfers, see pages 83, 88, 96 and 119; gel medium transfer, see page 97.)

Alternatively, by simply artistically altering original images—or copies of original images—you can also integrate them onto the pages of your journal, right alongside your doodles and your written thoughts. The ability to add photos or images from your life and to combine your various artistic creations on one page enables you to make your art journal completely personal and significant to you in every imaginable way. I hope these pages from my art journals inspire you to use transferred and photocopied images in your own artistic pages laden with personal meaning.

Image transfers

TRANSPARENCIES

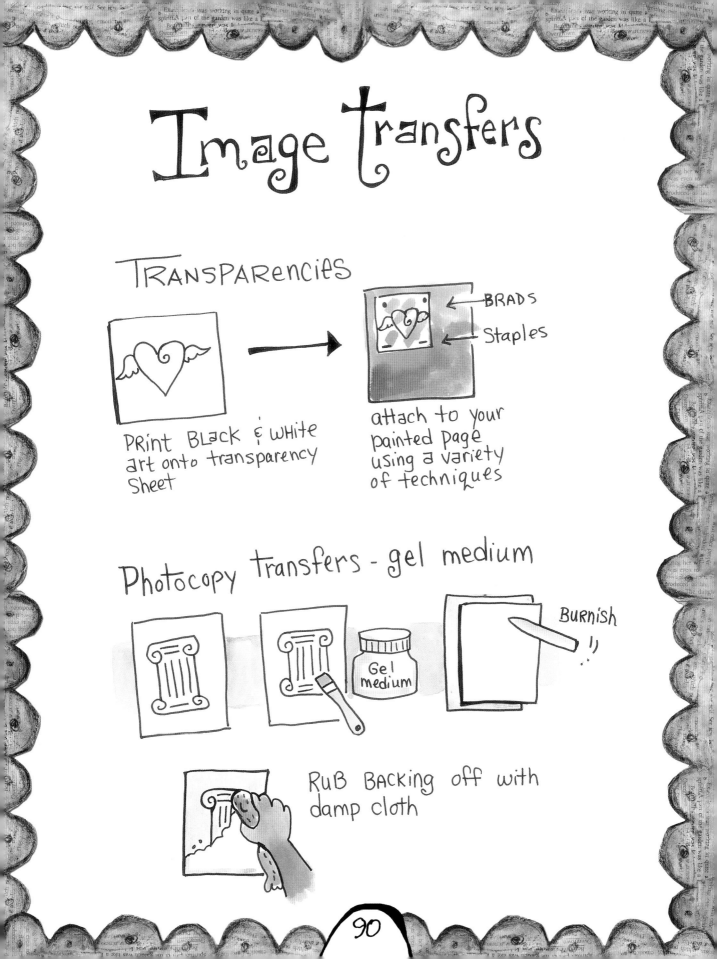

BRADS

Staples

Print Black & White art onto transparency Sheet

attach to your painted page using a variety of techniques

Photocopy transfers - gel medium

Gel medium

Burnish

Rub Backing off with damp cloth

Packing tape transfers

tape

Photocopy of Image

Burnisher

Cover image with tape

Burnish
Burnish
Burnish

Place image in water

Soak for 20 minutes

Peel off Backing

Hooray! You are now ready to use your transfer by mod podging it onto your backgrounds.

Image Transfers

← Packing tape method
I like this one the Best!

← Don't try this at home!
I applied the gel medium and immediately began removing the image.
As you can see it didn't work out too well!

✔ After waiting a few hours for the transfer to dry I was able to carefully peel away the white backing. Doesn't the dyed paper towel look cool peeking through the image?

Photocopy a photo
of a face, cut out
and glue to page.
Color with water
Soluble oil pastels,
Smudge or use a
wet brush to move
color around. ADD
dots with gesso.
Collage patterned
Papers around
face.

Color face with
watercolor pencil
crayons.
Embellish with
Patterned papers,
measuring tape,
glass marble (flat),
wire and fibers

Stuck on YOU!

Staples

Brads

eyelets

cello tape
and masking
tape

Trim

JOY!

Tags

Sequins

Joy

Zippers

Bottle caps

Marabou boas

Sprinkles

Paper clips

Safety Pins

95

♥ Cupcake heaven ♥ ♥ ♥

Sensual pleasure, pleasures... A lot of sweets, brightly wrapped... my open hands. All I saw of the...

The JOURNEY is
the
destination ⟶

Journal Bliss

Focus on the journey, not the destination. Joy is found not in finishing an activity but in doing it.

∞ Greg Anderson

"Are we there yet? Are we there yet?" How many times have you heard this or uttered it yourself? I have found myself, in my infinite impatience, saying this for much of my life. The thing is though, that when we're too focused on where we're going, we miss so much along the way— the serendipitous magical stops where we find incredible parts of nature that we would have missed had we not, say, been curious about a sign mentioning a park. Recently my partner and I came upon tufas (magical limestone turrets) by and in a lake simply by following a sign that beckoned us. It was getting late and we wanted to get to our hotel, but we resisted the temptation to rush to check in, and instead stopped and wandered into a magical natural space during what turned out to be the most perfect time of day—that magical hour when the setting sun casts a butterscotch glow across the landscape. I gasped at the magnificence of it all. Imagine having missed this if we had hurried to reach our destination. Much of life is like this. We need to stop and appreciate where we are right now, or we might just miss a deliciously blissful, simple moment that will take our breath away or fully engage us. Honor where you are today, in process, right there on the pages of your journal.

On the following pages you'll find examples of some of my ways to do this, some with gentle guidance and journaling prompts for you, others for pure inspiration. I hope you'll discover that creating art is alchemy—like transforming baser metals into gold. Surround yourself with materials bought and found and begin sifting through the treasures, intuitively picking up what speaks to you. Lay them aside and begin drawing from your heart. Now put them all together to make a piece of art. *Voilà!* Alchemy! The experience of letting your intuition guide your art journaling can in and of itself be life transforming.

Gratitude Journal Page

"The earth laughs in flowers."

— e. e. cummings

An easy and satisfying journal prompt is simply to create a page inspired by things you are grateful for—whether it's a list, a traditional narrative entry, a visual representation of the good things in your life or (my favorite, as you know) a combination of approaches. What I have found is that even on rainy, miserable days when nothing seems to be going your way, there is always some small thing for which you can be thankful. Taking the time to recognize these silver linings is just one way to enjoy the journey rather than focusing on the destination. And creating a gratitude journal page is a good way to remind yourself to focus more on what is right with your life rather than what is wrong with it! Creating these pages regularly as a creative and maybe even spiritual exercise—perhaps every night before you go to sleep—is a good way to make both journaling and bliss integral parts of your life.

A list is my favorite format for gratitude pages. Lists are so accessible and unintimidating; they're perfect for those days when you just can't muster up the creative energy to journal your thoughts in sentence form. And they're not just for gratitude pages; try them for any subject you'd like. Lists are fast, fun and easy, and they might hold more meaning than you first suspect.

GRATITUDE

reative potential

My backyard swing

My bohemian tribe

The flowers in my backyard

Children's laughter

Herbal tea

Walks on the beach

Art, art and more art!

Mr. G

Sunshine on my face

My magic cottage

My kids Jessica and Ryan

WILDNESS and bohemian

Doodled Inspiration

"Doodling holds a lot of information."

— Mary Lapos

Joyboy began as a doodle. When innocent squiggles find their way onto your journal pages, try having a conversation with the doodles. Ask them their names and what they are all about. If you listen quietly, you may just hear the response.

My conversation with the Joyboy doodle first led to this visual representation of joy unleashed. For me, thoughts of joy inevitably lead to thoughts of the ocean. I am lucky enough to live near the coast, and when I'm seeking joy and solace I often drive the ten minutes down to the beach to breathe in the salt air, listen to the waves and replenish my soul. The waves wash away my fears and stress and rejuvenate me. So it was appropriate to put Joyboy in this symbolic setting.

Choose or create a doodled subject. If it had a name what would it be? If it had a color what would it be? What emotion does your doodle give off? Fashion a page around your delightful doodle, whether it be a person, animal, plant or inanimate object. Have fun with it!

Journal Tribute

> "First comes thought; then organization of that thought, into ideas and plans; then transformation of those plans into reality. The beginning, as you will observe, is in your imagination."
>
> — Napoleon Hill

The pages of your journal do not have to focus on your own self-expression alone. Try creating a page that commemorates, pays tribute to or tells a story about someone whom you admire, someone who has inspired you or touched your life in some way.

At around fourteen years of age my friend Susan—who was painfully shy and gawky—decided to reinvent herself. During the summer of her fourteenth year, she was on a mission to transform herself from an ugly duckling into a beautiful princess. That year she watched the movie *Georgy Girl* and witnessed the remarkable transformation of the main character from homely girl to lovely teenager. She also read biographies of women like Barbra Streisand who were not thought of as traditionally beautiful but somehow were able to find the beauty inside and make something of themselves. My friend drew pictures of herself as she would like to be, made lists of the qualities she wanted to have and convinced herself that she would fake it till she made it. Soon she convinced others of her beauty and confidence, and eventually she believed in it herself. It's funny: When I hear Susan's story, I realize that we can indeed create our reality by seeing ourselves as we would like to be rather than wishing and hoping for something that is always out of our reach. We can be that which we desire to be right now!

Try creating a journal page that honors and celebrates, both in artwork and in words, someone important in your life or someone larger than life who has in some small way influenced you—even if you've never met. Some examples from my own journal are on the following pages.

ONE SUMMER SHE DECIDED TO RE-INVENT HERSELF. NO LONGER WAS SHE THE UGLY...

It all Began with

TWIGGY

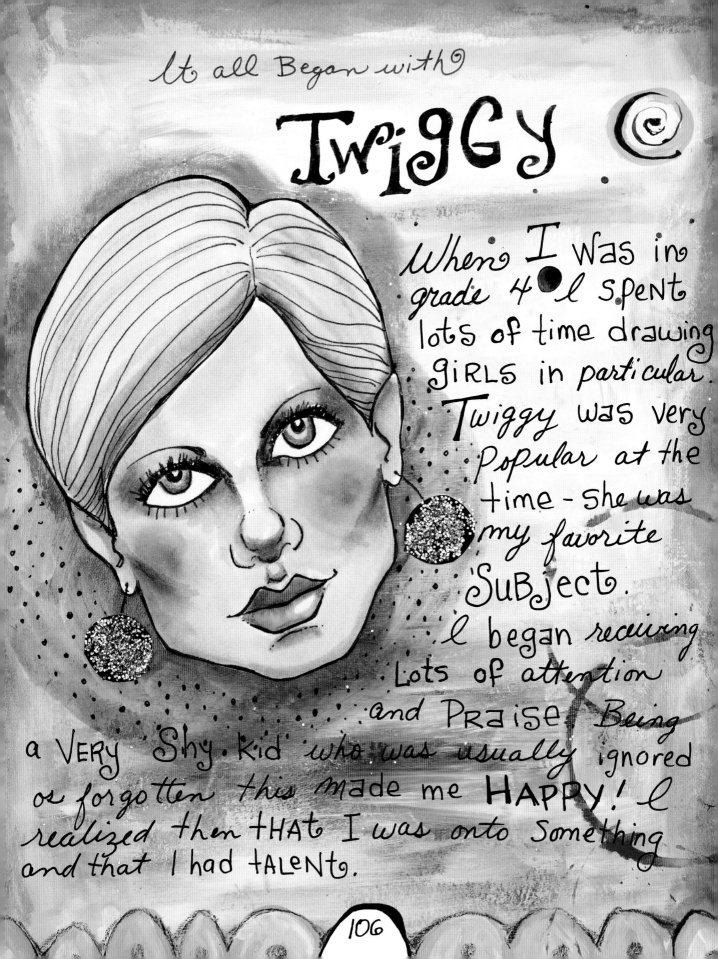

When I was in grade 4, I spent lots of time drawing GIRLS in particular. Twiggy was very popular at the time - she was my favorite SUBject.

I began receiving lots of attention and PRAISE. Being a VERY shy kid who was usually ignored or forgotten this made me HAPPY! I realized then tHAt I was onto something and that I had tALENt.

My Little Zen Masters

My two children, Ryan and Jessica were my first real teachers. They taught me all about unconditional love, all about acceptance, patience and of course being in the moment. From them I learned how to stop and smell the flowers, watch bugs endlessly and get lost in a world of imagination. Through them I was able to recapture a part of my youth and also experience the things I was not allowed to experience as a child due to having a fairly strict upbringing. Their night time fears of scary dreams and things that go bump in the night reminded me that it is okay to be fearful and to be comforted when you are afraid. Jessica and Ryan gave me so much pleasure as children that I still go out on adventures with my little friends.

Dig Your Magic!

"Dig your magic" means: uncover or excavate the magic that lies within you. It may be lying dormant waiting to be discovered but it is there nonetheless. How do you uncover your magic? By remembering that which excites you, knowing the skills you have that you excel at. What makes you stand apart from everyone else? Is it your writing abilities? Is it the ease at which you throw a party together? What truly makes your heart sing? I have a friend whose joy comes from singing karaoke on friday nights. If she wanted to further her joy she could expand on this and take singing lessons. What can you do to expand on your joy?

Symbolic Stories

> "To become truly immortal, a work of art must escape all human limits: logic and common sense will only interfere. But once these barriers are broken, it will enter the realms of childhood visions and dreams."
>
> — Giorgio De Chirico

Another way to tell the stories of your life on paper is to choose a pertinent story from someone you care about and relate it to your own experiences in order to realize a deeper connection on the pages of your journal.

The origin of this visual journal page is a story about my mother as a teenager. She desperately wanted a strapless ballgown and a room of her own. She wanted to escape a life of poverty and scraping by, and she felt that if she married, then she would be able to afford these simple dreams. Sadly, she never did get that coveted ballgown, but my mom's story reminded me of finally getting my own strapless gown when I was in my forties. My daughter, Jessica, and I were shopping at a vintage clothing store, and I spied this splendid cream-colored ball gown with tulle and extreme poofiness. Impractical, maybe, but it was calling my name. So I tried it on—but it was so snug that I couldn't get out of it. I struggled and strained but to no avail. I called the sales clerk over and I explained my dilemma. He said, "Oh, don't worry. Just do whatever you need to do to get out of it!" So I ended up tearing the darn thing! Now, this next part I simply cannot believe I did. I decided to buy the gown, but brazenly said, "I'd love to buy this dress but it's torn. Could I please have a discount?" The sales clerk who had advised me earlier smiled at me and deducted ten dollars from the cost. I was reminded of a favorite quote by Wilhela Cushman (a fashion editor, naturally): "Just around the corner in every woman's mind—is a lovely dress, a wonderful suit or entire costume which will make an enchanting new creature of her."

Can you see that life is simply full of blissful journaling fodder? There are so many endearing stories that enrich our lives and can be brought to life visually with a little creativity. What symbolic stories can you tell on the pages of your art journal?

THE STRAPLESS BALLGOWN

When she was a teenager

She always wanted a strapless

Ball gown

individuation

She thought to herself,

"When I get married I'm going

Have a strapless gown."

She never did get the gown she

Had only dreamt of.

XO

Anecdotal Journal

"It is art that makes life, makes interest, makes importance."

— Henry James

Not all journal pages need to hold deep meaning or start with symbolic intentions. Try taking an everyday anecdote from your life and illustrating it visually in your journal. Then add words in a stream-of-consciousness fashion, without censoring yourself as you go.

This page is a good example of this technique. A couple of years ago a woman I knew let me stay in her yurt (a sort of circular, domed, portable tent) on Salt Spring Island. I was pretty jazzed about it—except for the part when I would have to sleep with the resident feline, whom the owner claimed was a very spiritual cat. Odie was really not a cat. He was more like a person who had taken up residence in a feline body. I am not a cat person and have never owned a pet of any description. Sleeping with a cat was not right up there on the list of things I wanted to do. Yet there I was with Odie—who decided to sleep on my chest the entire night. Odie stared deeply into my eyes, and I swear he could see into my soul. It was incredibly disconcerting. Needless to say, I didn't sleep a wink! But it did make for a fun journal page.

Odie the Devotee

A couple of years ago I was fortunate enough to sleep in a yurt on SaltSpring Is. One of the conditions of sleeping in the yurt was that I had to *"love up"* the resident cat named Odie the Devotee. You see Odie is a very sacred cat but I am not a cat person! So I'm sure sensing this dear Odie tried to change my mind. He slept on my chest and stared deeply into my soul... he made me blush! anyway I didn't sleep a wink all nite what with the loud purring and the soul penetration. ~Yikes!

being petrified ← me

Last Day on Earth Prompt

"Some may think that life is laughing at us! Well we'll see who will have the last laugh!"

— Siro

I often wonder what I would do if I knew it was my last day on earth. How would I act differently, what would be important, who would I want to spend time with? Often the questions we ask ourselves can make excellent prompts for pages in our art journals, and this question is no exception. This page is my illustration of how I would spend that fateful day. Of course, my mom features in it. I immediately thought of how she's funny (rather old world) in matters such as reminding us as children to put clean underwear on since you never know if you're going to be hit by a truck. My sister is well versed in proper etiquette (something I never received a memo about! ha!), hence the sending a thank-you note as I'm about to exit this great big, beautiful world! I like to revisit this drawing every couple of years to see how it changes.

What would you be doing, saying or thinking if you knew it were your last day on earth? What other questions do you often find yourself pondering during your daydreams? Create a visual representation on paper. Revisit this prompt often.

I give you my heARt

Sometimes I feel as if I have Nothing
to give except for my heARt... after all
the MOSt valuable thing one can give is
LOVE

You can give love by giving Someone flowers, offeRing a Smile Running er-ands, making Soup foR thoSe Who are ill.

Show Love by planting flowers, paying for Someone's Parking meter volun-teering at an animal Shelter oR woman's transition house ......

Be gentle with It!

LISTEN

My Soul is Speaking to Me...

TICK

So i'm not really sure what i should be doing. Robert says i need to squeeze the tube every day. I made a collage today for Bev But apart from that I have not been too creative. i have been doing some affirmations for Abundance, prosperity, peace, joy magic. I know i need to trust that the universe wants me to succeed but every time then i begin to panic. Maybe i'm not trusting enough. also i'm asking the universe for the relationship... Not a "perfect person But a perfect person that i know and who i can in turn help now. Everyone tells me that i'm asking for too much!

Holding Peace. Creating magic. Being Love

Just Be

sitting by myself...

cocoon

BLOOM PEACEfULLY

FOLLOW YOUR BLISS

Violette

I have about 20 or more books on the floor beside my bed. ⊙ They are full of inspiring and encouraging words✶ that keep me going and happy!

i seem to be able to draw & write a lot at Whitby's Café since it is right on the beach & i really enjoy the atmosphere. People congregate there to meet for coffee, discuss Metaphysics and just... ♪ HANG!

Hanging out at Whitby's Café

STRESS...

i find my reaction to stress rather interesting. Instead of speeding up and doing things more quickly i slow down...go for a coffee or retreat to my bed for a short while and think about life.➤

The light has Been
The Secret is...
Within you All along!

CHAIR at WHITBY's Cafe

I wonder how many people have Sat upon this chair. Who has left their energy on it? Artists, musicians, store clerks, Students, house-wives?

a Forsythia branch... a wonderful Sign of spring after our long WINTER. It's quite lovely...this little sprig... Just bursting with joy. I think if I had to express joy without words I would do it with a flower

CReating when i let go i can connect with the divine & things flow.

What Does My HeaRt Say??

Just DoODLE

Magic Cottage

My name is Violette. I live in a purple magic cottage near the beach. Why is it Magic? Because I made it that way - I fill it with LOVE, good friends and family, whimsy and CREATIVITY. I paint my stuff with juicy colors and add lots of glitter! Won't you come and PLAY with me ?

Violette is a Creative Spirit who lives in a PURPLE MAGIC cottage with MR. G - aptly named for his tolerance of GLITTER found in food, clothing and some of the STRANGEST Places! Violette's art has been featured in Books, magazines, newspapers and television WORLDWIDE

BLiSS

She follows her "BLiSS" by inspiring others to Embrace who they are By teaching WORKSHOPS on Visual Journaling and Collage. Violette can BE Spotted near the quaint Seaside Community of White Rock, BRitish Columbia.

miss U has 2 Wonderful grown Kids - Jessica and Ryan

KNOW YOUR Life's MISSION

Glittergirl Van

Magic Cottage

Violette

One of My Painted Doors

The Doors of PERCEPTION

For a complete list of my favorite inspiring resources, visit my Web site and blog at www.violette.ca. In fact, I invite you to visit often and become part of a community of creative spirits! Wherever your journey takes you, may all of your adventures be filled with Bliss, Joy, Love and Happiness!

Index

Expand your creative horizons with these blissful North Light Books!

Wide Open
Randi Feuerhelm-Watts

Open yourself up to a whole new way of looking at yourself, your world and your art journaling. The *Wide Open* book and deck set is all about challenging yourself to take your art to the next level. The set includes 50 idea cards featuring mixed-media artwork on one side and thought-provoking instruction on the other, plus a journal for recording your ideas and artwork.

ISBN-10: 1-58180-911-5, ISBN-13: 978-1-58180-911-4, 50-card deck in a box with accompanying journal, 64 pages, Z0653

Journal Revolution
Linda Woods & Karen Dinino

Overthrow your inner critic's tyranny of fear and rules, and discover fresh techniques and inspiration to rant, whisper, beg, stomp or sing your truths. Celebrate your rough edges with a revolutionary new approach to art journaling, as you learn to vividly express your uncensored emotions and boldly record your deepest secrets.

ISBN-10: 1-58180-995-6, ISBN-13: 978-1-58180-995-4, paperback, 128 pages, Z0950

Creative Awakenings
Sheri Gaynor

What if you could unlatch the doors to your heart and explore dreams you haven't visited for a very long time? *Creative Awakenings* is the key to opening those doors by using art making to set intentions. You'll learn how to create your own Book-of-Dreams Journal, and then you'll master a variety of mixed-media techniques to use within it. A tear-out Transformation Deck will aid you in setting your intentions. You'll also get inspiration from twelve artists who share their own experiences and artwork created with the Art of Intention process.

ISBN-10: 1-60061-115-X, ISBN-13: 978-1-60061-115-5, paperback, 144-pages, Z2122

Living the Creative Life
Ricë Freeman-Zachery

What *is* creativity, anyway? Where do ideas come from? How do successful artists get started? How do you know when a piece is finished? Author Ricë Freeman-Zachery has compiled answers to these questions and more from 15 successful artists in a variety of mediums—from assemblage to fiber arts, beading to mixed-media collage. This in-depth guide to creativity is full of ideas and insights on what it takes to make art that you want to share with the world, and simply live a creative life.

ISBN-10: 1-58180-994-8, ISBN-13: 978-1-58180-994-7, paperback with flaps, 144 pages, Z0949

These and other North Light Books are available at your local craft retailer, bookstore or online supplier, or visit our Web site at www.mycraftivity.com.